What to Expect when having Expectations

Using the anger of unmet expectations to find peace

Ben Winter

What to Expect when having Expectations

Using the anger of unmet expectations to find peace

ISBN-13: 978-0-9992944-4-4
LCCN: 2020900763

Copyright © 2020 by Ben Winter.
All Rights Reserved.

Chapter 1 – Who

Chapter 2 – What

Chapter 3 – Those

Chapter 4 – Rules and Laws

Chapter 5 – Positive Expectations

Chapter 6 – Where

Chapter 7 – How

Chapter 8 – Fear

Chapter 9 – Regret

Chapter 10 – Go Forth

Appendix – Other Examples

> **"The only reason anyone gets upset is because an expectation hasn't been met."**

The subject of expectations and everything covered in this book is like a puzzle. To assemble the picture we have to start with each piece of the puzzle, describe the individual pieces, and then show how they fit together. While reading, keep in mind that each chapter is a piece of the puzzle and may not make sense in regard to the previous chapter, but I promise, the picture will come together by the end.

Chapter 1

Who

this book is for

A lot of readers first ask,

"Why should I read this book?"

Let me answer that with some questions of my own.

Do you want to reach your goals?

Do you know why you aren't reaching those goals?

Do you really know why?

Do you get upset in your life?

Do you use that upset moment as a positive trigger to get what you want?

Do you know how to use the upset?

If any of these questions sparked interest, you should read this book.

Chapter 2

What
expectations are

Expectation. The word that often sparks a negative thought when people hear it. Why? We'll get to that later.

What if I told you that we have been looking at expectations all wrong? What if expectations aren't negative?

ekspek'tāSH(ə)n

Expectations are simply a belief that something is going to happen. This isn't good. This isn't bad. This is a neutral statement about a belief. You can expect good things to happen. You can expect bad things to happen. The expectation coming to fruition isn't good or bad either. It is simply a thing.

Expectations set a framework in which those involved can work with each other and create an understanding so that they can accomplish more together. Think of a contract. A contract is simply a set of expectations between two or more parties.

Is there ever a time where we don't have some kind of expectation?

We expect the sun to come up in the morning and set at night. We expect there to be oxygen to breathe at all times. We expect the things we left next to our bed at night to be there when we wake up. We expect a thousand different things before we even leave the house in the morning. Yet, many of you don't understand that these thoughts are happening every moment of every day. Any time one of these obvious expectations is met, we simply move on without acknowledgement. This is totally understandable and there is nothing wrong with doing so.

By the way, acknowledgement of these good things is a simple form of gratitude. It isn't as strong as being grateful but a step in that direction. Acknowledgement is, being in the present. Seeing what is right in front of you at the moment. Feel free to read "The Power of Now" by Eckhart Tolle for more on being present.

Expectations are simply a thing. Not good. Not bad.

Chapter 3

Those

who don't think they have expectations

There are people who say, "I don't have expectations so I can't be disappointed".

Just know that this thought is in-and-of-itself an expectation. This means you have expectations in not having expectations. Stop lying to yourself.

Expectations are unavoidable.

Just remember, if you get upset at ANYTHING, you had an expectation. And it went unmet.

If you say, "I set my expectations low so that they are easier to meet", again, if you have ever been upset, you had an expectation that was unmet.

Some people think of expectations as Future Resentments. Well, as you'll see from reading this, that is a choice, not a direct result of having expectations.

Basically, get over it. You have expectations. IT ISN'T A BAD THING.

Now that you know you have them and that they are unavoidable, let's move on.

Chapter 4

Rules and Laws

are expectations

Expectations, rules and laws, set a framework for us to work in. And this is a good thing.

Rules and laws are forms of expectations. Rules and laws are expectations with consequences should that expectation go unmet. Someone getting a speeding ticket shouldn't be upset. They knew the law (expectation) and they knew the consequence (expected result of breaking the law). The reason they're upset is because they had an expectation of not getting caught. Or they felt justified for their action, like they are better than everyone else at driving. Again, they have an expectation of being better than those who get tickets.

Sports. A prime example of written expectations. Each player, ref, and coach knows the rules and is expected to play by those rules. And when they don't, there are expected consequences. When the rules are followed, the spectators can see a game with expected actions that result in points being scored.

If there wasn't a set of rules, then we would see something resembling a sport, but have no idea if everything is copasetic.

One player could show up in combat gear, another in a tutu, one has a ball, the other has a knife, and one shows up in a stadium, the other hiding in the mountains. Who the hell knows what should or shouldn't happen? Might be fun to watch the first time, but at some point it would get boring and suck. Even the players would get bored because they don't know how to play or how to win or if they were doing a good job at whatever it is they were supposed to be doing.

Think of kids playing a game and every time they don't like the result, they change the rules. It sucks. As an adult we get bored really fast and stop playing with the child because it is a brain aneurism waiting to happen.

From this perspective, expectations of what the game is, how it is supposed to be played, what happens when the rules aren't followed, all make for a much more interesting experience for all. When a player does something amazing while following the rules of the game, we are in awe of them. Amazed by their talent. And are blown away by their achievement. But this is only possible by having a set of boundaries to work in.

Part of my background is doing stage improv. And if you don't already know, stage improv has a set of rules. Expectations of each and every player on stage. Yes, improv has rules. These rules for stage improv actually apply to everyday life as well. What we do, every moment of every day of our lives, is improv. We don't have a script. This means that knowing and following the rules of stage improv in our daily lives makes life easier and more fun. We can succeed easily. Rules, simply stated, are expectations that people agree upon. They agree that this is what we should or shouldn't do as well as what happens when we do or don't follow those rules.

Why bring up improv? By learning improv you can have an easier time with communicating expectations. Expectations work for you and against you when it comes to improv. They work for you if you have the expectation that the other improvist are following the same set of rules. It's a reasonable expectation for sure. If they are, then the performance will be a success. If they aren't you can at least expect that you will follow the rules and come out successful regardless of those around you.

Expectations don't work when you aren't focused on the present. If you expect the scene to go one way and then it takes a completely different turn, your expectation goes unmet, you get frustrated, and you get lost. It takes too long to get back into the scene and you may lose everyone in the process, including yourself. So, improv helps you to practice reasonable expectations as well as staying in the moment so that the expectations you have, that don't serve you, lose control over you.

Known vs unknown

We are often aware of our expectations. These are expectations we have vocalized to ourselves and those around us. Contracts and rules are known expectations. Meeting with friends at a specified place and time. Getting the food you ordered the way you ordered it at a restaurant.

Laws are known expectations. They are written down, understood, voted on, and set in place. Think traffic laws for starters. A group of people had to sit down, decide what would work best for a situation, like an intersection, and what the rules should be for that scenario. And now that it is agreed upon and made into law, we agree to follow that law when we request a driver's license. We buy into the law by association. And we must if we want the license.

Contracts that we sign to buy a house, lease a car, and have insurance are known expectations. True, we don't always read and understand everything in those contracts, and yes, that can lead to an expectation being unmet, but it was in there.

We can get upset having known expectations. I for one really hate it when people aren't following the same traffic laws that I am following. I mean, we all took the same tests. Or was mine way more thorough than others? Not likely.

When our friends leave us hanging at the bar far beyond the time we agreed on, we get upset.

But…

It is the unknown expectations that really get us upset. Most of the time, we didn't know we had these expectations until we got upset by them not being met. I love the example of a married couple and the wife asks the man to take out the trash.

Simple request. "Honey, please take out the trash." Polite. Well mannered. Reasonable. He even responds, "Okay dear". But then what happens?

He sits there, watching the game, and doesn't immediately take out the trash.

Well, now she starts to wonder if he heard her. But rather than say anything, she lets it go for another hour.

Time goes on and he still hasn't taken out the trash.

She starts to get a little upset. She doesn't understand why he isn't doing this simple task.

But why is she getting upset? Did she have some kind of expectation she didn't know about, or better yet, didn't vocalize? Yes!

You see, she didn't specify **when**. She expected him to do it right away. But did she know she had the expectation until she saw him not doing it right away?

It's possible it was one of those expectations that is so common to her that she forgot to share it.

Now we are stuck. She is upset. He has no idea that he did anything wrong. She wants to scream. He wants to watch his game. He knows to take out the trash. She knows he isn't doing it.

But now that she knows she is upset, she can do something about it. More on this later.

Chapter 5

Positive Expectations

and why we won't be talking about them

This book is not going to talk much about positive expectations. These are the expectations where we expect a positive result and then get those results. People simply don't acknowledge these situations as expectations because they got what they wanted. Positive expectations are great! No reason to dwell on this or think much about it. It's already getting us what we want, so why bother changing it? No need.

I expected to wake up this morning and have a hot shower. And I did. I can acknowledge this. I can be grateful for this. But for most of us, we just carry on without a second thought.

So, let's move on to what isn't working and make sure we know how to switch it around.

Chapter 6

Where

expectations come from

Why do we get upset from unknown expectations?

First, let's explore where these unknown expectations come from. They come from our past. What happens in our past? We learn things. We learn how to walk, talk, use silverware, who to like, who not to like, why we like or dislike them, how to be polite, how to be an asshole, and so on. We learn habits and views of the world, mostly from our parents, friends, schools, and society. This past creates our subconscious perspective on life. It teaches us what to expect without thinking about it. These are also called "programs".

You <u>expect</u>, without thinking, that you will use a fork and knife correctly when you eat. And you do - without thought. Except when you accidentally stab yourself, and then, of course, you get upset.

You expect, if you were taught to be racist, for the race you hate to cause problems. Because of that expectation you immediately fear them when you see them even if they aren't doing anything close to what you expect.

By the way, if you are reading this book I hope you know that there is only one race when it comes to humans. There are different colors of humans. Different cultures of humans. But ultimately one race.

Our past, our expectations or *programs*, our subconscious thoughts all lead to <u>unknown</u> expectations - meaning, sometimes we don't know what programs we have until we get upset by them going unmet.

Unknown programs (our subconscious) create situations

that cause us to be upset, because we may want something that is known (consciously) that contradicts the unknown program (subconscious).

For example: you may want to be wealthy, but your paycheck is minimal. You want something different than what you are getting. Your subconscious, or programs, dictate your pay because of your beliefs about yourself, what you are worth, how much money you should make, and so on. And when you want something new and different (conscious thought) that goes against your programming, you have an internal fight about what is and what "should be".

Let me pose a simple question. Do you like being told that you are wrong? Probably not. Most people will fight for years to be right when they are told they are wrong. Just look at politics.

Do you mind it if you figure out you are wrong all on your own? Probably not. You might fight yourself and the situation for a few minutes, but then you are okay with the end result. You figured it out on your own.

Your subconscious is primed to always be right. It doesn't know the difference actually. It just knows what it is supposed to do.

Think of a computer that was programed to compute 2+2 as equaling 5. We know that is wrong, but to that program, it doesn't know any different. In fact, no matter what you type in or how you try to reason with the program, it will always think 2+2=5.

Your subconscious thinks it is right about what it knows. This means that when something goes against your subconscious, it will fight to be right. Your subconscious runs thousands of thoughts a minute. You can only <u>consciously</u> think about one thing at a time. That's a huge discrepancy.

The good news is, if you concentrate on that new thought for a prolonged period of time, it becomes the new program. It's called creating a new habit.

If you want something different, you have to fight the subconscious thoughts that have been running you for years with constant conscious thoughts until your new reality becomes your past or your new subconscious. And hopefully with enough conscious thought towards what you want, the new programs function more efficiently than the old ones. The old ones don't go away, but the new ones will become stronger.

I used to have zero self-confidence. And that program still runs to this day. But because I have done so much work on myself, it is basically a starving program locked in a closet with little to no power over me. And the program that says I do have self-confidence is much louder. It's out in the living room, cheering me on every day.

When you want something that you don't have, we call that a dream or a goal. And the reason you don't already have it is because of your programs.

When you want your dream or goal you have to consciously work on the steps and thoughts to get you there. This is the hard path. It is hard. You have to work at it consciously, day by day, until it becomes your new normal.

The easy path is simply to live each day the same as you always have. Wake up, go to work, come home, do some stuff, go to bed. You'll get a result. You'll have a future. It just won't be your dream. It won't be your goal. And likely you will be upset because you had an expectation of reaching your goals and dreams.

It can be hard to get what you want. And the simple reason is that you are constantly fighting your internal thoughts, your subconscious, your programs every time you want something different.

Let's look at loneliness.

Dictionary.com defines loneliness as, "sadness because one has no friends or company". More often than not this stems from our own thoughts, feelings, beliefs, and actions and NOT because of what actually is. People have a perception about friends and life. This comes from their childhood. This comes from society. This comes from experiences. And it becomes unconsciously propelled in our day-to-day lives.

Stay with me here…

Remember, people don't get upset unless an expectation hasn't been met. As I said, we all have expectations about the future. About things that haven't happened yet. We have expectations of how future events are supposed to come to fruition. These future expectations come from our perspectives. Our unconscious thoughts.

Stay here just a bit longer…

People don't want to be wrong. We will do anything and everything we can to be right about what we believe. We will turn to people and situations to confirm our beliefs so that we can be right about them.

And here is where it comes together…

If our past experiences lead us to believe that we "aren't likable" and that becomes our subconscious thought, then we have an expectation moving forward that people don't want to be around us so that we can be right about our perspective. We exclude ourselves from situations to confirm that belief. To be right about it. We don't see the signs where people are including us. We ignore *facts* to be right about our beliefs. Remember, **this is all subconscious thought**.

What can you do about this?

Number 1: Awareness.

Be aware that loneliness is a perception based on a program. A subconscious thought that doesn't serve you.

Number 2: Focus on the present.

This is similar to awareness but is more moment by moment. Awareness is knowing that you have a program running. Focusing on the present means that you look for opportunities to challenge your preconceived ideas of friendship and how people look at you. How to be included.

Number 3: Create a new reality.

If people aren't inviting you to events, invite them. Figure out something fun to do that most everyone enjoys, put in the effort to make it happen, and reach out to people. You'll start to see who doesn't shy away from you. This is a step in creating friendships.

Number 4: Follow up.

When you do something with someone, follow up with them. Show them that you care. But go easy and tune into their expectations. Don't be creepy. Instead, just send a text message or an email saying, "Thank you for coming last night." Some might call this step, appreciation. Again, you don't want to overdo it and prove your "unlikable" program to be right again. We have a funny way of sabotaging ourselves like that.

Number 5: Consistency.

You have to do these things again, and again, and again. At some point, the people you have been inviting to do things will invite you to do things. They will start seeing you as a friend. And more importantly, you will set a new program in place that says that you are likable.

When something like loneliness comes from a subconscious thought, you have a lot of work to do to overcome that program. It wasn't created in a day, it won't be solved in a day. Give yourself a break and practice the steps.

I had several situations happen to me as a child that, to this day, shaped my relationship with friends and dating.

The first was right around 9 years of age. Elementary school. I had two friends who I did everything with. We played during recess, we went to each other's houses, we had sleep overs, and so on. I was invited to one of their birthday parties and the next day at school, they both beat me up and threw my backpack over the fence. My friends betrayed my trust. First situation for me to create a program that I am "not-likable" and not to trust people.

Looking back at it as an adult I can see that the one kid whose birthday it was, was jealous because his mom spent extra time and effort on me because I was a picky eater and didn't want the food everyone else was having. I got special treatment and he was acting out because he wasn't getting that treatment on a regular basis. As an adult I can reflect on that story and see a different experience. And though it doesn't change my subconscious, it does help me create a new story in which I can strive for something different.

My next experience was in middle school. A friend I hung out with almost daily, decided to steal from me. While he apologized and gave me the item back, I knew deep down that he did it maliciously. And I knew he wanted to get away with it. Here I was again, being betrayed by a friend. Another notch in the "not-likable" subconscious score card. And another moment of don't trust your friends.

As an adult I know that he was simply looking for attention. His mom was never around. She was a single mom attempting to make ends meet. He was alone, and doing bad things was probably the only way he got attention from her.

When it came to dating, I had many opportunities to find out that I wasn't likeable - for my subconscious programming to prove itself.

When I went to summer camp for the first time I got a "girlfriend". Basically she was the girl you sat next to at the fire and occasionally held hands. That's about it. She happened to be my first kiss too. Even though it was a dare, it still counted.

Well, the following year it was time for another camp girlfriend. I was rejected by 3 girls in one week. Talk about setting in a program! I don't think I asked anyone else any year after that one.

In high school I didn't attend prom. I asked one girl because my friends kept pushing me to, but her parents said she couldn't go. This means I got to be right about not being likable.

And college was not much different. I simply put myself in situations where I didn't even see the potential for dating or even see that I was liked until it was too late.

Don't worry…I broke out of my shell and turned it all around. Yes, I still sabotage myself in relationships. I see it. I work on it. I still have work to do on myself.

As long as we are breathing, we have work to do.

Ever have an obsessive thought?

What are obsessive thoughts? I used to have obsessive thoughts about improv shows that I have done. Recounting what I could have done. Why "I sucked" at something. Feeling like I failed during a scene. Likewise, when dating, there are thoughts of "what if" and "why aren't they texting back" and so much more. Those thoughts just kept running through my head.

It wasn't until I realized, after making a huge mistake with one person I was dating, that I was never right about the "why". My obsessive thoughts about it actually caused the relationship to fail.

So, what are obsessive thoughts? **Brain Conflict.** It comes down to two things: programs and expectations.

First: Programs.

As stated before, programs come from past experience. We don't want to be wrong about what we perceived in the past so we make sure that we create similar situations in the future to prove that are programs are right. This becomes our belief about what is, was, and will be.

Second: Expectations.

To reiterate, we don't get upset unless an expectation isn't met. If our programs contradict our expectations, we obsess over the scenario because our brains are in turmoil.

From the dating perspective, someone may have been really bad at dating and their past has proven that they simply "aren't lovable". It becomes a subconscious decision that they didn't even know they created. They keep having relationships that prove that they aren't lovable. And now, when a new relationship comes along that looks promising, our expectations of something being different comes into play. This goes against our subconscious thoughts. Now our brain (conscious and unconscious) starts to fight itself. It's a problem that isn't easily fixed. And because we made a conscious thought, we are now constantly in battle with that unconscious undertone.

With improv, when I would remember a scene and tell myself I did it wrong, it was because a past belief that said: "I'm not good enough". It was subconscious for sure, but it made me question myself and the actions I took. This was a form of not letting myself know that I did the best I could at the time. And if I didn't do the best, at least I could learn from it and not beat myself up about it.

The one thing that really seems to take care of these thoughts is to simply be. Be in the present. Focus on the now. Stop the current thought and do something else. If you are thinking too much, then do something physical. Go for a walk. Go see a movie.

Being in the now is a form of being patient. In the case of text messages not being returned for hours, well, you just have to keep your mind occupied doing something else so you don't go crazy coming up with 1363 whys that aren't correct. Stop the internal fight so you can proceed with life.

When it comes to past thoughts about what was done incorrectly, by focusing on the present, you realize that nobody but yourself cares. And then you can consciously decide to just shut up about it.

I will be the first to admit that being upset happens even when you are working on yourself. In fact, it probably happens more often because you expect to be less upset by doing personal growth work. And then, when you don't magically change quickly, you get upset because it shouldn't be so hard. Well, I say, use the upset to your advantage.

BE UPSET
USE IT
LET IT TRANSFORM YOU
And here's how…

Chapter 7

How
to use the upset

Being upset is a trigger for something great to happen. It is a point where we can choose to do something different. A point that can make things better for us and those around us. It is a point in time where we can choose peace.

Many of us know the quote by Einstein, "We cannot solve our problems with the same level of thinking that created them". One interpretation of this is that if the problem is emotional, you cannot solve it emotionally. You can solve it physically, spiritually, or logically.

Since, being upset is an emotional issue and not everyone is spiritual, and solving it physically can lead to bigger issues, let's solve this logically.

Here we have a flow chart of taking your moment of being upset and turning it into not being upset.

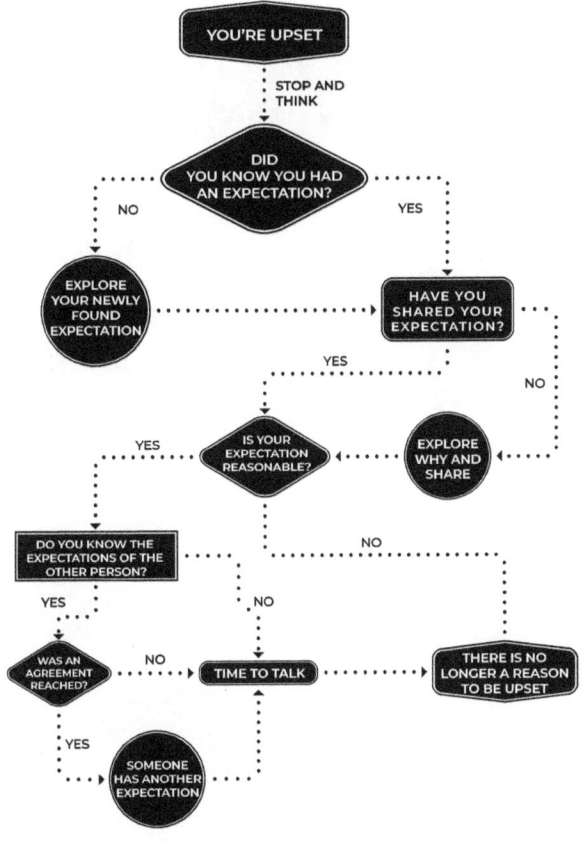

Let's walk through the chart in some detail.

As you notice, the first step is knowing that you are upset and taking a second to stop being upset; and this becomes the start of the process.

The first question to ask yourself is, "Did I know I had an expectation?"

I would say that most of the time, we didn't know. So, congratulations, you have a newly discovered expectation. You learned something new about yourself and now you can do something about it. You could feasibly go straight to not being upset now…but let's keep going down the path anyway.

Explore your newly found expectation. This part is extremely important. Explore this newly found piece of yourself. This new expectation. Examine it. Figure out where it came from, why you have it, what it means, and who it is for. This could be one of those programs that came from your childhood that no longer serves you.

From finding out you had a new expectation, the answer to the next question is pretty obvious, "Have you shared your expectation?"

> **HAVE YOU SHARED YOUR EXPECTATION?**

Since you just found out about this expectation, the answer is most certainly "no".

It doesn't take much to understand why you haven't shared it. You didn't know about it. So, that's easy enough to get past. But is there another reason?

It is possible that you didn't share because of some fear. More on this later.

And since you have been examining your newly found expectation, you can ask yourself if it is a reasonable expectation.

If not, then why are you even upset? Time to move on. But if it is reasonable, how does it compare to the other person's expectations? Do you know about their expectations already?

> **DO YOU KNOW THE EXPECTATIONS OF THE OTHER PERSON?**

Or is now a good time to start a conversation? And let's say you do know their expectations but you haven't shared your newly found expectation?

It would be reasonable to say that no agreement was reached. That your newly found expectation is neither known nor agreed upon. This means it is time to talk with the other person, gain clarity, and it is no longer reasonable to be upset.

If you did know about their expectation and they knew about your expectation and you both agreed on your expectations but someone is still upset… someone has another expectation.

If this is the case, then it is time to go through the workflow again, talk, and stop being upset.

What this boils down to is COMMUNICATION. In today's world we actually suck more at communication than ever before. We have so many tools that put words in front of people, but words are only a small part of communication.

I love the movie "The Invention of Lying" because people say exactly what they mean and share all of their expectations with one another. And yes, it is uncomfortable to watch at times because we aren't used to being so honest.

Remember that communication is more than just words. This book isn't nearly as effective at conveying this information as if it were delivered in person. This is because communication is only 10% words.

As we know from text messages and social media it is easy for us to write something to someone with little to no fear of what we write. But if we had to say those exact words to someone's face, it would be super hard and there would be a lot of fear about sharing those thoughts and feelings. But why?

Remember the trash scenario? The wife has no reason to be upset when we explore this flow chart. She only shared the expectation of what she wanted. She didn't share why. She didn't share when. She didn't ask him about his expectations. And they didn't come to an agreement. There was virtually no communication. He isn't innocent here. He could have also asked the why and when questions when she made the initial request. Both parties are to blame. There was no communication.

Whoever gets upset first has the upper hand - if they stop and think.

They can go through the chart and come up with a way to communicate more effectively.

They can, by being upset, become the instigator of peace.

Chapter 8

Fear

There is a section on the flow chart that seems small yet holds a HUGE amount of information. It is the NO line that comes off of the box "Have you shared your expectation?" This NO line is huge because not sharing an expectation means you have a fear around it. You might fear that it will scare someone away. You might have fear that it is unreasonable. You might have fear that you don't even believe the expectation yourself, and you now have to start questioning everything about yourself and your beliefs.

Fear is an expectation that something bad is going to happen. We have all had those times where we expect something bad to happen and then it does. Then we get to be right about it. And most of the time this is subconscious. Our programs get to be right, again.

This is one of those opportunities to choose differently. What if your newly found expectation is a deal breaker for a relationship. If you don't share it with your partner, negotiate, and come to an understanding, can you seriously continue in the relationship without regret, resentment?

It is the NO lines in this chart that hold the most opportunities for growth and self-exploration. This is where awareness comes into play. Awareness of what is happening. Awareness to know that we aren't proceeding because something else is holding us back – likely a fear of something bad - an expectation of a negative outcome. Awareness is the key here. Just like becoming aware of being upset is a trigger for change, becoming aware of why you aren't sharing your expectations is just as important and possibly an even bigger opportunity for change. And for the better.

Boundaries

People often want to share with others what their boundaries are but are afraid of sharing those boundaries. Do you have a problem with saying "no"? If so, you aren't sharing your boundaries, a.k.a. your expectations of how others treat you. And likely, how you treat yourself. Sharing those boundaries can be scary. But as so many quotations say or elude to, if people don't want to respect your boundaries, do you really want them in your life?

Yes it is scary to speak your mind. But at the end of the day, when you do, you feel better about the person living in your skin.

You won't grow old and have regrets about setting boundaries.

You could grow old and have regrets about NOT sharing your expectations and setting boundaries though.

Chapter 9

Regrets

What do regrets and expectations have to do with each other? Easy. Regrets are unshared or unrealized expectations. I read an article in Forbes[1] about the 25 biggest regrets in life.

Most of them certainly hit home at some level. And a lot of them had to do with unmet expectations of ourselves. A lot of them are even unknown until they go unmet and it is too late to do anything about it.

One in particular goes back to boundaries, *"Getting involved with the wrong group of friends when I was younger."* How often do we attempt to fit into someone else's expectations of us rather than choosing our own expectations of ourselves? You know what? Yes, you will lose that group "friends" but you will either bring some of them along who don't want to be there either or you will find new ones. It's called taking a leap of faith.

This one, "*Not having the courage to get up and talk at a funeral or important event*" is one I want to address. But first I want you to think about an important event at any time in your life where you spoke your mind to one or more persons.

Believe me when I say it takes practice to speak your mind. And those people you know who speak their mind are intimidating to many. Intimidating people are only intimidating because we see something in them that we don't see in ourselves, yet it is there. It is available to us. We can do what they are doing. Sometimes it is best not to do those things (a bully is not one to imitate). A world renowned speaker at the front of a room of 1000 people - they are intimidating to most of the observers. But guess what? You could be there too. You simply have to give yourself the boundaries to do it. You have to have the courage to try and try again until you get there. You have to start and fall on your face. You have to practice going against your negative self-talk for a long period of time. You have to keep at it. And as long as you keep going and keep going and give it your all and never give up on that new boundary, you WILL NOT have any regrets.

I may not have written the best book in the world, but I wrote it. I shared my thoughts and beliefs on a subject. If I dropped dead after writing this, I would have no regrets about sharing a little piece of me with the world.

I often think of death and what I would have left undone. I do so much more now, and speak my mind more, and set boundaries, and share my expectations, so that I have so few regrets when that day comes.

I want to show my son what it is like to live a life of no regrets. Will I succeed? Maybe. I don't have an expectation that I will be a perfect parent. All I can do is my best and know that when my time comes, I can say that I did my best. And know that I am not lying to myself about doing my best.

Remember though, about regrets, that sometimes we don't know we have them until the end. This is just another example of an expectation we had that we didn't know that we had until we get upset by it going unmet. And yes, sometimes it is too late to fix being a parent of a young kid when they are full grown. But you know what? You are still alive. You have time to do something. If that is you apologizing and sharing your thoughts and feelings with your children, then that is something you can do.

It is never too late to go back to school and get that degree.

It is never too late to pursue that one relationship. To repair a relationship. It's never too late to forgive.

Forgive yourself.

Chapter 10

Go Forth

If you are reading this book, there is still plenty of time for you. Time for you to live your life the way you want. For you to have more joy. For you to spend less time being upset and more time having fun. More time for you to mitigate future regrets.

You have the power to change. It is a choice. It is your opportunity for you to consciously choose something new until it becomes your new subconscious.

Don't wait for someone else to change you. That person doesn't exist. Again, there is nobody on this planet that can change you.

Until you choose to change, those who will support that change will not appear. And they will only support the change. They won't do it for you.

This book gives you one simple how. Using the upset. Will it work for you? Only if you choose it to work. Are there other ways? YES, a thousand times, yes. "How's" are the mechanism for change. There are infinite "how's". You just have to have the intention and conviction for change. Use as many mechanisms as you can to implement that change. Noticing when you are upset and using this book and its flow chart is just one of those ways that might make other "how's" much easier.

Go forth and live life. Choose something different today. Choose to change your next upset into peace-of-mind.

Appendix

Other Examples

Let's explore some other examples of being upset from expectations, such as:

- Religion

- Life with a roommate

- Driving

- Sex

- Politics

- Work

- Raises

- Science

Appendix Examples

Religion

When it comes to religion we are typically exposed by our parents to a religion when we are young. When we learn a religion at a young age it becomes another program that we live by. Some learn about heaven and hell. For others, there is neither. And if it is taught that there is a heaven then it is also taught what takes you there and what keeps you from there. These teachings ultimately create a subconscious belief (a set of programs) that affect us and how we operate in life.

When we grow up and see that other people don't believe what we believe the conflict begins. Meaning, those who don't believe what we believe are inherently saying to us that we are wrong about our belief. Not because they say so, but because if someone doesn't believe what we believe then they believe something that possibly contradicts what we believe. Hence, immediate feedback that what we believe isn't correct. Or, conversely we see them as being wrong. This fires off the upset one way or the other. The expectation that if we believe something, everyone else should too because it is "right". It's only "right" because that is what we were taught at a young age and it is what our subconscious believes to be "right".

Let's jump straight to the box in the chart that says, "Is your expectation reasonable?"

In my opinion, it isn't. There are so many religions on this planet. There have been wars fought to prove one religion is better than another. Yet all of those religions remain. There is no way to prove which religion is correct. There is no way of knowing how a religion came to be. Yes, it has been "written" in books and scrolls, but if the game of telephone has taught us anything, the original message from many thousands of years ago, has been long forgotten.

We try to justify this lack of understanding by holding on to a simple set of beliefs.

And that's okay. **Be at peace with your beliefs.**

If you have to force others to believe what you believe then you are looking for validation of your own beliefs and you aren't at peace with those beliefs. Being at peace with your beliefs really and truly means being okay if you are the only one who believes it.

My belief is that nobody has it all fully understood. There is no way we, as humans, with our collective thoughts, could possibly understand what created this vast universe. We simply cannot comprehend it. It's too vast, there are too many questions, there are too many unknowns.

I also believe that the two things that are found in every religion are the only thing we really need. Don't be an ass and give. Or better yet, just be a good person.

Again, this is my belief, I am at peace with it, and I need nobody else to agree with me.

Appendix Examples

Life with a roommate

Whether it is your significant other or a roommate in college we each have our favorite way of doing things. And maybe not our favorite but our only way of knowing how. Often times it's our schedules and timing of things that fall under those unmet expectations. Maybe you grew up cleaning the house once a week and that's what you expect of yourself and those around you. What if your roommate is on a two week schedule? Or what if they grew up without having a schedule and just did it when it felt like it was time? The simple fact that you grew up in different houses with different parents, there are going to be some unmet expectations. It simply WILL happen. Even if you grew up in the same household with a sibling and then moved in together after college, you are going to see the world differently. Maybe one of you adopted the schedule of your youth. But maybe the other decided it wasn't for them. Now there is going to be some unmet expectations. Just because you are used to how things go and how they "should" be, doesn't mean that there shouldn't be communication about your expectations of one another. Living in close proximity demands constant communication and check ins. If you aren't coming across a known or unknown expectation almost daily, you aren't paying attention.

Will it always be like that? No. If you talk through them as they come up, then they will be resolved over time. You will understand each other so much more. And you will have reached many agreements about each other's expectations. It can become a beautiful thing.

And yes, you are going to have to share some of those things that spark fears. It can only get better for you when you share. By sharing you won't have regrets later in life. If sharing means you end up moving out, I am positive you will be happier down the road.

And if sharing brings you closer together, then that is a super bonus and oddly enough, expected.

Appendix Examples
Driving

My hot button. Driving. Drivers. The road. At some point we have all yelled at someone in another car or called them out for being an idiot or not knowing how to drive.

Many of my frustrations come from watching people do things that are illegal. I mean, we all had to take a driver's test. We all should know the rules. So, when people drive through a dead stoplight without stopping, or honk at me when I do, I really question our driver's license system. I have been broadsided by someone who decided that they should have the right-of-way for a dark intersection when all they had to do was stop for a few seconds.

And this is just a prime example of how our perceived knowledge from our youth drives our subconscious on what is "right" when it comes to the road. We took a test and had to know things about driving to get a license. It isn't unreasonable to believe most people passed with enough knowledge to not be a danger to the road. Maybe I am wrong about how to treat dead intersection lights. Or maybe my perception of the law is correct. Either way, my subconscious says that the other drivers who don't stop are a problem whether it is right or not.

One main source of all of our slow traffic, merging. I expect people to know how to merge and to let people merge. It requires both parties to make it work without someone having to slam on their brakes.

But, are my expectations reasonable?

No.

No, because I am unable to communicate those expectations with every driver on the road.

Unless I was a billionaire and spent all of my money on ads, and even if I did, there is no way to reach everyone. And even if I did, other drivers couldn't share their expectations. We couldn't come to an understanding.

It is simply a lost cause.

Needless to say, I go through the workflow almost daily when it comes to driving. The good news is that I don't get upset for very long anymore. One deep breath and I am back to dancing and singing as though I was the best at both.

Appendix Examples

Sex

If there was ever a subject where we could all use a little more communicating, this would be it. In our world today so few people talk to their kids about it. Kids today don't have sex-education like we did when I was young. Some kids receive scare tactics as their sex-ed.

Why we wouldn't talk to each other more freely about something that nearly everyone on this planet does regularly is beyond me.

Why we wouldn't talk and communicate with our partner is even crazier to me. Who better than the one we are having sex with.

If you want to talk about unmet expectations, let's talk about sex.

Maybe you grew up thinking it was only for procreation and your partner learned differently. Someone is about to be very disappointed in the bedroom. Or both people.

Sex is something where both parties simply have to share their expectations and then be willing to come to agreements regarding those expectations. Some people like pain when it comes to sex.

Some people can't associate the two. Some don't want to cause pain to the other person and can't physically bring themselves to do so.

Some people want simple one position sex. Other's want every position possible. But if you don't communicate your desires and needs, then your expectations of your partner will go unmet. You will be unhappy. You might even fight and argue. And then there will be no sex. Ever hear of a sex therapist? They are there to help guide you through these unspoken or even unknown expectations. They facilitate communication. And yes, they also find the underlying cause (programs) that are running those expectations and explore where they come from, why they are there, and if they serve you in what you really want.

Expectations around sex are generally reasonable. And should be communicated. The best sex I ever had was after communication about what we both wanted. Amazing how a little conversation made sex better.

In terms of sex-ed for our youth, yes, we should be communicating.

We should share the good, the bad, and the ugly. What to do, what not to do. Just because you saw it in a video, doesn't mean it is the norm, doesn't mean that you shouldn't talk with your partner and ensure they are okay with it.

We should be communicating what happens when you have unprotected sex. Yes, the good, the bad, and the ugly.

We should teach respect and understanding. Not just scare kids into never having sex and not enjoying it when they grow up.

We cannot expect people to know anything good or bad about sex without teaching them, communicating, and sharing expectations.

And yes, there may be times when an expectation causes that relationship to fail. But what if you find something better as a result?

Or better yet, what if you share your desires (you never would have known without sharing an expectation). Now you just opened the door to better sex and better communication.

Appendix Examples

Politics

Democrat, Republican, Independent, etc…Oh how this world is full of unmet expectations. And if you want to see people fight to be "right" about their beliefs, you need not look any further than politics. The truth can be plastered on the walls in front of their faces and they will fight about it. They will make up some crazy stories as to why they are right. And no, not one side is innocent here.

Back in the day, when the United States leaders wrote the constitution they communicated their expectations and came to agreements on those expectations.

Since then there has always been someone who wanted to see those agreements in a different light. Interpret them differently. And skew them to match their beliefs. Their programs.

For some reason, in today's society, so few politicians are willing to admit to themselves, let alone others, that they were wrong about something. I believe they have coined the idea of changing your mind as "political suicide". But what about peace-of-mind? I for one would rather be at peace and not have a future career in politics than to fight everyone to be right about something when the evidence points clearly against my belief.

Unfortunately, ordinary American citizens suffer the most because a few politicians don't want to explore their unmet expectations, to communicate, and come to a mutual understanding. They would rather fight than communicate in a meaningful way. And there is no winning side when this happens.

All we can do is educate ourselves. Learn for ourselves. And not just from one news source, but many sources. We need to decide that we are "right" or "wrong" on our own - not by what the media tells us is right and wrong.

If it helps you, my rule of thumb is this, the more adjectives used to describe someone and/or a situation, the more opinion it is than news or facts. It's at least a starting point to ask questions and better educate myself on the situation.

Appendix Examples

Work

Oh work. The place we go to earn an income. The place we go to accomplish tasks. Our home away from home. The people we spend most of our time with. Yes, more time than with some of our family members.

People don't want to do something that isn't at least comfortable. Ideally fun and peaceful. Yet most of us experience some level of upset when it comes to work. Examples: A coworker not pulling their weight; a boss not being reasonable on a project deadline; a client wanting the impossible.

So many things can cause us to get upset in the work environment. And for some work environments, it is career suicide to share those emotions or show them to the world. Even sharing things on social media could get you fired.

So what do we do? Use the upset as a trigger to figure out where you are, what your expectation is, who is involved, and schedule a meeting. Have a conversation.

I highly recommend not having a conversation where you start by making the other person wrong. It should be more about sharing your understanding of things and wanting to get their side of things. This shows them what your expectations are, and you can hear from them what their expectations are. Then, when you both realize you are not on the same page, you can start communicating and coming to agreement.

Sometimes you will see that being upset at work is unreasonable or has nothing to do with work. You can communicate with yourself and come up with an agreement with yourself. You can stop being upset and move on with your day just by taking a second to explore what is going on for you.

Appendix Examples

Raises

Speaking of work, we have expectations around raises too. I'm going to share my story about just such a thing.

I had been in a group at work for a couple of years and did pretty good work. I had been with the company for about 5 years at this point. I knew that every year we would get some standard 3% raise. It happened every year.

Then I decided to ask for a non-standard extra raise because I thought that if anyone deserved an extra raise it was me because of the amazing work I was doing.

Well, my boss told me that I had had a complaint against me by another employee and that I would need to go 6 months without another complaint before such a request could be considered. Okay. The expectation I made up is that if I am good for 6 months I get a raise. The expectation of my boss was unknown. So no agreement was reached.

Six months went by and I ask again. Well, yearly raises were right around the corner (probably 3 months away) and he told me just to wait and he would see what he could do.

Well, happy recession time came and "nobody" got raises that year. Nobody got fired, but nobody got raises. I was upset because I had been asking for nearly a year and felt I had been jumping through hoops. I understood the logic though and let it be for another 6 months.

A little before that 6 months, our company was bought by a bigger company. And when I approached my boss he said that the new company was going to be auditing where people were vs the median pay for similar jobs, and that a correction was likely. Ha! I bought into it. I did my research and I was due for a BIG increase because I was grossly under paid for my position. Turns out so was everyone else. We all were under paid. And so nobody got an increase. Or at least that was the excuse I got.

After almost 3 years of trying to get a raise I quit. I left the company and went into business for myself.

I had unmet expectations about a raise. I was upset I wasn't getting one. I did communicate some stuff but not enough and ultimately left the situation. There was no longer a reason to be upset with them when I am no longer there.

What I learned about myself after leaving, is that while I was there, I had a bad attitude. I wasn't personable. I showed my emotions and spoke my mind. Career suicide. I didn't do it the right way. I learned that my communication style didn't work for everyone. The person who filed a complaint about me did so because I was short and to the point in my email communication and it came across to her as though I was angry with her. This, of course, was her perception to the email, how emails should be, and she didn't ask me if I was angry with her. I chose at the time to answer the email with a simple and clear answer rather than fluff it up nice and neat so that she would feel good about herself after reading that email.

I had an expectation that a simple, concise, and accurate email was acceptable and that nobody should take offense to them. I just saved us both time and energy.

And maybe my expectation was reasonable, but it wasn't agreed upon by the other party. We never discussed it.

I have no control how someone perceives an email. Written communication lacks inflection. Had she read that email with the intended inflection, it would have been a non-issue. But since I could only control me, then I could have chosen differently. I have no reason to be upset at my past because there wasn't any communication between the parties involved about the situation. But I could have a conversation with myself about the situation. I can resent my past or I can learn from it. I choose to learn from it.

We all have an expectation about compensation when it comes to work. This is why so many people leave their position for a different one - to be paid more. There are definitely other reasons, but compensation is definitely a big one.

And if you aren't willing to talk with your boss and come to an agreement on how to get paid more, then you can't expect to get paid more. You have to share those expectations.

Appendix Examples

Science

When it comes to science the facts are the facts. So why is this an area of contention in the world? Because people don't want to be wrong.

I find the beliefs of "flat-earthers" to be a joke. The science, the facts, the images, everything is there that proves the earth is a sphere. It just is.

When I read a theory from "flat-earthers" that says why it is flat, I assume that what is ultimately running them is the pure desire to not be wrong. If they admit to the earth being a sphere then they will lose all that they know. They won't have their friends who also believe what they believe. There is fear to losing your friends because you might not get any new ones. I get it. Being wrong simply isn't fun. But it can be super freeing.

I have a problem with one branch of science – statistics. Often statistics are shared to prove something. One thing, I learned in my college stats class is that "correlation is not causation". Yet too many times we see a graph and decide that the information shared and shown is the truth because there is a graph showing us why it is true.

One stat that always makes me laugh: 95% of all car accidents happen within 5 miles of your house. Okay. So, with that in mind, once I get past 5 miles I am very unlikely to get into a car accident. Yes!!! Road trip.

Oh, wait. Correlation is not causation. Because guess what else happens within 5 miles of your house? About 95% of what you do on a daily basis. Meaning your chances of an accident are the same no matter where you are. It's a statistic to share a point, not a fact.

I expect our scientists to be truthful. To only share the absolute truth. And I am sure that is what they strive to do. So when I see a study about a controversial subject, I always ask about who is funding the research? Why? Because the data can be skewed so that the statistics of that data "prove" a point.

We can easily show a graph that says that the decline of pirates has been the reason for global warming. Meaning, as the number of pirates in the world has decreased, the global temperature increases. So it must be that pirates kept the global temperature in check. That's asinine. But you chart it out and tell people it is true and is statistically accurate, it must be true. Yet any intelligent person would question that statistic and rightfully so. We should question all statistics. That's one thing science is supposed to do. Question things until there are no more questions.

All too often people assume that because they heard a statistic or saw a graph that it must be true and accurate.

In my youth I subscribed to just such a thing. But through education, I realized that I can take the information given, add on to it, question it, and make my own judgement. Yes, I could probably have a conversation with someone about what they see and come to an agreement or a better understanding. But I rarely get upset when it comes to science. Mostly because I know that some of my expectations aren't reasonable. And mostly because I am unable to discuss those expectations with the parties involved.

What does upset me is when there are facts that are irrefutable and a grown adult doesn't want to be wrong about the opposite. Take global warming. The only "science" that opposes it comes from scientists and data that are funded by the companies that have the most to lose. They have statistics skewed in their favor.

But again, it is unreasonable for me to be upset. I don't have the means to have the necessary conversations with those involved. And even if I did, they are so set in being right that we would likely never come to an agreement.

I'm not saying I won't do something, but there is little to be upset about while doing what I can.

Thank you for reading. I hope this book brings a new tool to your tool box for ways to find peace in life.

I highly recommend taking improv classes as they help with keeping you in the present. It is a great way to manage expectations, play with life, have more fun, and create a new way to communicate.

You can read more about improv and how it can improve your life at successimprov.com/blog

Citation:

1. https://www.forbes.com/sites/ericjackson/2012/10/18/the-25-biggest-regrets-in-life-what-are-yours

What to Expect when having Expectations

Using the anger of unmet expectations to find peace